You Envelop Me

Also by Laynie Browne

Poetry

The Complete Works of Apis Mellifera, with Bernadette Mayer, Further
     Other Books, 2017
P R A C T I C E, SplitLevel Texts, 2015
Scorpyn Odes, Kore Press, 2015
Amulets and Letters, Belladonna #173, 2015
Lost Parkour Ps(alms) & *Psaumes De Parkour Perdus*, Presses Universitaires
     de rouen et du havre, 2014
Roseate, Points of Gold, Dusie, 2011
The Desires of Letters, Counterpath Books, 2010
The Scented Fox, Wave Books, 2007 (winner of the National Poetry Series)
Daily Sonnets, Counterpath Books, 2007
The Desire of Letters, Belladonna #93, 2006
Original Presence, Shivistan Books, 2006
Drawing of a Swan Before Memory, University of Georgia Press, 2005
     (winner of the Contemporary Poetry Series)
Mermaid's Purse, Spuyten Duyvil, New York City, 2005
The Desires of Letters, g - o - n - g editions, 2005
Webs of Agriope, Phylum Press, 2004
Nascent Toolbox, with Lee Ann Brown, The Owl Press, 2004
Pollen Memory, Tender Buttons, 2003
Gravity's Mirror, Primitive Editions, 2000
The Agency of Wind, AVEC books, 1999
Clepsydra, Instress, 1999
L O R E, Instress, 1998
Rebecca Letters, Kelsey Street Press, 1997
One Constellation, Leave Books, 1994
Hereditary Zones, Boog Literature, 1993

Fiction

Periodic Companions, art by Noah Saterstrom, Tinderbox, 2017
The Ivory Hour, Spuyten Duyvil, 2013
Acts of Levitation, Spuyten Duyvil, 2002

You Envelop Me

Laynie Browne

OMNIDAWN PUBLISHING
OAKLAND, CALIFORNIA
2017

© Copyright Laynie Browne, 2017. All rights reserved.

Cover Art by Noah Saterstrom
Natchez #1
Acrylic on paper, 9 x 12 inches, www.noahsaterstrom.com

Cover and interior set in Electra LT Std and Garamond 3 LT Std

Cover and interior design by Gillian Olivia Blythe Hamel

Offset printed in the United States
by Edwards Brothers Malloy, Ann Arbor, Michigan
On 55# Enviro Natural 100% Recycled 100% PCW
Acid Free Archival Quality FSC Certified Paper

Library of Congress Cataloging-in-Publication Data

Names: Browne, Laynie, 1966- author.
Title: You envelop me / Laynie Browne.
Description: Oakland, California : Omnidawn Publishing, 2017.
Identifiers: LCCN 2017020700 | ISBN 9781632430380 (paperback : alk. paper)
Classification: LCC PS3552.R748 A6 2017 | DDC 811/.54--dc23
LC record available at https://lccn.loc.gov/2017020700

Published by Omnidawn Publishing, Oakland, California
www.omnidawn.com   (510) 237-5472   (800) 792-4957
10 9 8 7 6 5 4 3 2 1
ISBN: 978-1-63243-038-0

for Patricia Browne, in loving memory
1942 – 2011

And I am walking in her garments
In rooms made of pollen and chance and noise
Towards the errors in humanism
— Lisa Robertson

Contents:

Owl Pages

1

Say goodnight to a page, petting morning
Fetching listen— to plumage
Move with no sound
Perch— the view from above is
also the name of the dress
If only I could find— could find
ninety feathers spare
Will listen to your voice and know
her color or form synonymous with
Her name is— say goodnight —
action, what will be anyone's future
Protector from crush and velvet-hued wing

2

Crave the color of not at all burnished
Held, fancied, stewed, stained
blemished, burning, borrowed
Crave the color of cracked and borrowed ice
Garb that does not fit like a tourniquet
Beak-ed, like a troubadour, tawny
Incisors or vise grips within, please
protector, protect— her —accompany
our— occupy, escort us with sound
providing vintage, hand-drawn guides to—

3

If an owl flew over warriors before a battle
They took it as a sign of—a sign of ascendancy
She kept a watchful eye on —a sign of— Athenian trade and
commerce from the reverse side of her coin
If you walk around an owl in a tree—copper tree
it would turn and turn its head — how is it possible
for her to twist — to watch you until it wrung
Past and past participle of ring
It rung— a horizontal support for a foot
Whose own —a sign of— her copper— book

4

We've been inside an owl's egg
Begged to solve for perimeter
protection against drunkenness
—owl— stolen from rose
An eraser borrows your brain
I give you a powerful mantra
but how not to swallow the copper coin twist of—
she, Athenian at prow of copper tree thinks in
swatches of— color and form synonymous
Not needing the ninety odd feather
twist of it all, that used to be
owls' eggs, cooked until they turn
to ashes improve eyesight

5

If she recasts a passage it is whatever— she says it will be

Long-eared and venerated, despised and admired

How long can this go on, her knowing everything?

Outside— light muddy— veil slips— watchers of—

The owl flew with absolutely no sound

Large, brown, landed in copper eucalyptus

A bat and an owl in the same breath

Same branch indicates ownership of —

Owl claims ownership of that thought location for

night vision, chamois of prophecy

Protector from forces that could pull

a person into guardian waters, locations for—

If she recasts a passage of water it is— an owl on a rock above

6

An owl was once a girl
Watcher of the dark
Germination, tender of all underground
peaches, russet bird in green bower
Songs of dripping infrared
Blind in daylight she was both deceased and
— so the bird turned
A newly released—night
A newly interim russet, water beetle
Newly released, and ultimately pure air

You Envelop Me

16

for I have taken refuge in you

A book —whose wings— swallow me

Bird, created from water mixed with sand

Uses of wings, and claws hold oil for lamps

Conceiving a wing-ed book is beginning to sort one's thoughts

An egg placed under the foot of a bedframe— to steady

Quills for writing were unknown in Talmudic times

Birds of three hundred and sixty-five hues read

Headlines or psalms as an indistinguishable combination of

Affliction, concentration and praise

"Flee as a bird to your mountain."

32

When I kept silent, my bones wasted

You envelop me

After death animus hovered around the body
An owl climbed outside one's form
Quintessence— in a great treasure-house, or cage, a columbarium
May only move through human frames
In the fourth heaven— lake of birds— continually praise
Affirm ardor in the shape of doves
Causal birds in the Acherusian lake were consulted
As advisors upon creation of humanity

41

You set me before you

Sparrow and swallow rise upon
walls, usher where sung
into hidden prefigured
crown adorned with nest
Preoccupy a sanctuary of the future

42

My tear has been my bread

Your billows and Your waves
have gone over me

                        No act was undertaken
       without advice of
              augury, prophesying

Open a window
              among Chaldeans, Greeks, Romans
that the breath may

              augur = avi-gur, οιωνος, οιωνισται
              sing, whisper

     "for a bird of the air shall carry the voice, and that which hath wings
              shall tell the matter."

59

A refuge in the day of my distress

Divination by means of weasels, fowl, and stars,
Who is an enchanter?
He, for instance, who says:
My bread fell out of my mouth
My staff out of my hand

Divine by behavior of the fish
Snake and cloud omens
An owl alighted on the tree against
Which you now lean

Who speaks the language of flight?

Do not advise, even in whisper
birds carry a voice   on

77

You held fast the lids of my eyes

and your footsteps were not known

For one minute each day
the comb of the cock turns white
Not a single red stripe is to be found
He stands on one leg

No fly alighted on the table of the prophet

He foretold his end from the sighing of the tamarisk-tree

Who speaks the language of trees?

90

A dwelling place you have been

before mountains were born

Recalling a verse early
in the morning is a prophecy
in miniature

"Thine ears shall hear a word behind thee, saying,
This is the way, walk ye in it."

The voice must be an unusual one
desert in mouth — city in womb

Last weft of the dying propelled
across loom by hand, as divination

105

seek presence continually

from the divine mouth

Hydromancy
    ebb, colour
        scry, disturb the surface
           the spurious drown

                Belomancy
                    it is asked of me; it is forbidden
                        the arrow which flew the furthest
                        bears no inscription

137

upon the willows we hung our harps

Rhabdomancy

        rod, wand, staff, stick,
            douse
                 where they fall, bend, warp
                         in mineral sun and ore of moon

note: Poem numbers refer to psalm numbers and italicized text at the beginning of each piece is taken from that psalm. One traditional mourning practice investigated in this book, is the reading of ten particular psalms often identified as "Nachman's healing psalms." These ten psalms, nine of which are represented here, chosen by Rebbe Nachman of Breslov (1772-1810, Ukraine), exemplify his use of sacred texts as meditative tools, and highlight his religious philosophy which revolves around intimacy and direct conversation with the divine.

Mendicant: "Dear She"

She was not going to say, as she faced her beloved on the platform, about to lose her life: "you'll always—"

So much we could lie in bed and talk about as if we'd never been

Your arms rest on a countertop. Slander, an affliction on your person or house in the form of a whitish rash. How shall we say anything. Believable.

If these times were pretend—

When language has been ignored it becomes less needy, more abrupt and a cancellation effect is possible. I pick up a brush or an urn. To collect something. What becomes of the irretrievable?

Who becomes anyone then? If I have forgotten what I am here for, and the impatience which follows. You'll be away until—the end of several series of curses. I must be free to say anything. Last summer was too much travel for completion. I want all of the projects, even if still without proper homes, to sit on my shelves correctly. I want to know what is in every notebook and to disallow all unnecessary pages. I want everything in order, as if I were dying.

The one message which brings me close transposes the salutation so as not to say "dear she" but instead begins: Thank you so much "dear she." Does that make "she" more dear or do I imagine this hopefully? As if to make oneself more dear to another were reason enough to lift one's head.

The solidity and warmth of your arm upon a counter, and my sudden sense of you very much alive. We all inhabit each other —

And —all of the students in lectures while occupied on devices. Why are they there and— clicked away?

I was at radiation and I was annoyed because they were making me wait. I'd already waited half an hour and I had to give a talk in one more half an hour.

So I said, are you going to treat me? And I really thought that then I'd have to go give my talk— dead.

Your medicine is not my mendicant

Would you rather hike thirst or scour wells? Singe coats or go cold?

Would you prefer this portrait surgically installed?

Or would you prefer a non-surgical progression of pricks before your veins collapse?

And they said you shouldn't have another glass of winter

And technicians were rough assisting you off of the metal tableau

May I have my opiate vise now, she asks. And the radial engine says no, then wavers, consents

If only you'll sharpen. If only you'll share every numb sense

Anyone's grief is not my grief and your grief is not my loss and your loss is not the loss of progress, or ill-matched items one cannot do without.

She was becoming her other self and when failings re-emerged we placed them on a countertop. Then we hit them with a large mallet and we laughed. Or I should say, that is what we wished to do.

I also wished that the heroine in any book wouldn't look at someone so calmly and bordered. So you said, she should have said, "why don't you just show me yours?" And I said, "and instead of saying, please don't say anything more, and walking away in her bonnet, she should have said, *I want to walk in the rain.*" Also, they could have undressed in the garden. We could easily be expressive non-speech. A glance could do it and—we have barely time to succumb.

An Urgent Walk Across A Moor

Even though she breathes—

With permission

      sleeping— now

to go— anywhere

      Before someone else wakes her

Why not let—her

      wake to something —other
than—

Don't ask anything   —of her

She reclines at the edge of

Face turned inward —

— bed of angels

While someone lying there— not her but the one dying

What continues — uneven voices

Charts to measure — merely thought

Outbursts, places by the bedside

(a map- in three dimensions of wading)

Medication, whose?   —   tears

Not even circling in this cold— cold
Room today cold, window curtains drawn
Feeding her teaspoons of water, temperatures, promises

Await like a bed of always just imagined sleep
Don't pull her —from the steeping
Who is here, watching over the body?

We sleep through arguments' silence. We sleep
while mouths quake or ply. We sleep in shadow
through delirious glitter. We sleep prone, like

explosives closely fitted. Asleep in one another
None of these times shall we therefore believe sleep
as a strategy immune to this cold

In a photograph she stands beside a car
One brother and a farm, eyes bend a lake
As a teen she stands in a swimsuit in an empty field
In the background, an oil rig

Her smile awakens snakes, heat leans to look
She stands in wooden dress, beside flounced stove
Looking less like a child as she commands
From the opposite side of her own portrait
Siblings, barely born, her arms complete with them

Sleep on the living room floor which doubles for daytime

And when we return as if death weren't a part of —

We've cried enough, he says. Come again?

We walk and talk. We wish to be with her on the other side of this

I beg existence again of heavily lidded precipitation— driving through

Is this more or less dangerous than a four-year-old driving

Or an infant crawling out of a window?

Please allow her to rest
Lower your eyes and your courtesy and let her —
Lower your voice and stop flipping the
pages of her bedside
Don't ask about her gowned, throned
Are you cold?
Edits made at bedside where
we blink through everything wrong

We have so many beginnings and now
middles or middling, minutes or mittens

If girlhood is a beginning and maidenhood
a middle art, what of the 'wife' in midwifery

cloaked and hooded for her urgent walk
across the moor to an expectant mother

or to birth an opposite crossing

Her hemlines do not protect her anymore

than phials and tinctures she carries
under protection of — invisible —

She is so willing — miracle
of loss — middling

Burrowing into — displacing the unknown with
something so empty as to be blindingly solid

Opposite of ghost, thirst, hand, fathom
Middle art, listening, loaning, leading until

We might, at least precariously —
inexplicably, unseen until this moment,   light

Written At Bedside

What might be today. Sit down in something murky or somber, not setting by mouth.

Patch through angels of agitation. Pulling blankets and light not permitted.

Blue eyelids, haloed. Room vaults. Bed lurches. She dreams she is galloping on one foot and then found her other foot. She wants to be near a photograph of her grandchildren.

She wants us to stand in a line, doesn't want our mother hallucinating. Speak in the pure fountain you've become. Lip blue, like Shiva. Color of blue backdrop, blue necklace, assertion of veins.

Rub whose back she knows. Her blue lips beautifully part and rest upon a pillow.

Someone took her shoes, and then her water shoes.

Put them on your arms and you can walk through puddles on your hands.

How to die, he asked, rolling amid bedding, how do I?

Up wooden steps inset with the sound of the oxygen machine. I hope no one can hear me. Going out of her skin, she answers: *sedate*. It could happen suddenly, like awareness of a brook.

I couldn't say this any other way, such as in "I am you," a book falling, or suddenness. One child is afraid of fairies in the dark with flashlight but another three year-old-girl wasn't ever afraid. I listened to the sound of someone weeping underground. When you are a fount. A font. A sacred. Underwritten. Lying down.

Which blanket, blue or yellow? We don't need any water in our beds. Drink a courtesy of river.

We've been someone else. Angels aren't beckoning, merely present, gowned. We put words in your mouth like water, wet, cloth, spoon, unguent.

Sadness wasn't liquid. You held no pen. No memory of the levitating sculpture you call gladly mundane, an orchestrated timing, a body, a berth.

So you stand in a window framed, leaning out or longer-legged as if so quick to turn a head. So sick to turn a friend—a phrase. To take along a river, to curtain remembrance, to winnow. Where were you? You text me into the room— you use your thumbs as if I could write through this transition. She's looking at her shoes. She uses her work as a kerchief—a window— a page to draw over clouds. She uses her face as a mob, mop, hysteria. She uses the space— she tells me what to do— she dictates as if it were messier. She listens to the angels at windows— she checks the catheter— she sits on the green divan and waits. You thumb through where there is something or nothing in her hands.

The roses by her bedside, thumbing. The texture of the roses is insistent. She stretches out in the mouth of the flower. In and out of the room no matter who is in the corolla. She needs to own the disc or eye. She wants to whisper to the bedside, to work beside the lurch. The bedside tray isn't used anymore because she does not eat anymore. The mouth cannot see the straw and the small drops of water but the lips can feel. The feet are cut off yet still visible. They fling but are paralyzed. The bird outside the window knows nothing of the solitary room inside the rose. The bird inside this subject is not yellow but beyond color. The bird inside the window is hindsight and the bird inside her memory is flying. We'll fly and remember every phrase or step we ever took. It takes a long time to dance all the way back past her many treetops— can be seen from the window and light and air. Music frees more than I could ever locate inside a register of night made by the dark wings of birds inside your hidden eyesight.

Let's not be carried. Let's not do anything but sit here. Roll around and— how do I die? Now permission has been granted and she fears everyone else's death as if they were her. She says— My sister has died. The babies have died. My daughter has died in a car crash. Call an ambulance for my daughter who drove off — let's not do anything but be carried by wings. She sits on the couch and watches me. Waters something. Each she is simultaneous. She says. She is asleep now. Someone is dying. We must go to a funeral today. Whose funeral is it? We don't know yet, we tell her, but you can rest. Rest before you go anywhere. My fingers fly through her like the texture of roses. When my first child was born I listened and the space could be heard. Sacred space became splashed with sound and my child was bathed in the light of sound while I nursed him. Does anyone listening understand about the light of music? My child understands and begins to play.

I can sit by this window and by this bed and by my mother dying because my fingers and my life have been given to me. For how long is — naught. I am grateful for the room, for her radiance, even as she—. I can see her breathing. The white sheet rises and falls and the music makes everything —everything. We do not drown and we do not blink and we do not dream. The child pulls the crown over her head simply, as if it were made for her. It was made for her. Her light is the light of all life that breathes in and out of this room— that leaves one body and transfixes another.

I fall into a devastating love, so much so one cannot breathe or bear to be away. That one might die to be away. Every moment not enmeshed with the beloved is a moment lost, a moment anticipating drowning love. This is my remedy for death. The fingers of roses, the light of music and moments which must be enmeshed with the beloved. These are the haloes—nameless centers of circles and vows. Unfixed infinite of the rose: We taste the lover, hear her light, our hands are petaled, unfolding.

Now I want to change my mind— maybe loss is one blink in a maelstrom and this is another but the bedside isn't triple negative, that's just one lie. Our illusion is called "we take a trip to Scotland" or something else. Let's not get carried away with a long and beautiful title for our loss. We walk with image and thought upon dashes. She is a guardian and a giver. I am floating sadly somewhere and the music makes the room move. Every day that I am here I will write this and when she is gone so will my sentient words be gone— out to seek apparition.

Language means nothing to her now — a series of symbols she knows how to use but does not remember. Is she thirsty, hot or cold? I am watching the wind through the windows pull the molten yellow curtains. I am watching as rose laden surfaces sadden and weep. Language means nothing to her now. Would you like some water from a straw? That's enough. Just a little more. That's raising your bed and lowering it. These are your feet. She's finally resting.

"That was not sleeping," the beginning of a beautiful novel you know. I stopped reading his books because of the violence. The oxygen machine says 'concentration data.' The bed says 'montgomery marketing.' The bottle says 'one capsule by mouth.'

Mix those statements with ether. Lamp says, please be very quiet. Chair says, I'm thirsty for resting. Roses say, the kind of love not enmeshed with dark wings.

Written from her bedside. I'm so glad she can rest. She's herself, and otherworldly— who can weep? Who can sweep the ground like a curtained dress?

I have not written anything that happens or anything that has not happened. I have tried to describe the silence that isn't explained by thirst or pain, by sleep and concentrated waters. Rivers explain themselves.

September Shall Never End

To the funeral in your brain:

You are afraid to travel long distances so you do not read where the line
or the road is going.

Rewrite your town, staying nowhere until the procession passes.

If you leave during the three knocks your breath will be full of fireflies.

If you hear three knocks, and no one is there, someone close to you is —

It doesn't matter where they live, or if they are alive.

Don't hold your breath in a dream but agree to go everywhere in the rain.

If you see an owl direct it to a tall year in your memory tree.

Birds crash into my windows almost every day.

If your grandmother never played the piano in her living room, teach her

Two musicians in the family means that a third is sure to follow.

Cemeteries are the best place to walk while considering the future.

A bird through a chimney invariably disperses ash.

If you chill, up your spine, purchase a new, second-hand coat.

If a picture falls off the wall ask yourself, is this where I ought to be?
Take an artist to dinner.

If you spill salt crawl under the table gathering future tears.

If you love someone who has died, cling to the body, embrace the corpse, cut a lock of hair from her head, and once the body is removed, continue to speak to her every day.

In a house with only one door you come and go without considering another passage.

Keep only clocks which do not run.

A scissors for cutting flowers, a trowel for planting blooms. If both blades are broken mold a flaxen heart.

Burn a taper and train your eyes upon the flame to direct your wandering thoughts.

If you say the name Mary Worth 100 times into a mirror in a darkened room and she appears in the mirror, you are probably an adolescent.

If you eat an apple in front of a mirror and invoke the face of your true love you risk finding fault with yourself.

Look into the face of the deceased and you will notice that their eyes no longer meet yours.

If you should find a diamond-shaped fold in clean linen do not use a needle, bake bread or sow spines.

If your shadow wears shoes, and the moon appears red— remove your clothes, turn them inside out, put them back on.

If a white dove wears a necklace, and it breaks, pour bourbon into fire.

Touch a button, a snowdrop, red and white flowers in a vase. Hawthorn blossoms in your home are an invitation to the invisible.

Once land has been sighted, drop an umbrella upon the deck and allow weeds to grow.

Rest a broom infused with fragrance beside heated water.

Remove ashes from a stove, large drops of rain from sunlight.

Prick your finger on a thorn and stain the wings of a visitation moth.

Never speak ill of the living because they are very delicate and unpredictable.

Phoebis & Psaltria

A conversation {in waves} between butterfly and bird who follow a mourner

Of Yellow was the outer Sky
In Yellower Yellow hewn
Till Saffron in Vermillion slid
Whose seam could not be shewn
                    —Emily Dickinson (1676)

"If matter is trapped light, by seeing yellow flowers you restructure molecules, and you're not as solid"
                    —Mei-mei Berssenbrugge

Psaltria

I call you Cloudless because you are Cloudless Sulfur.

In color only, we match, though we've never been seen. Then how is it
we speak? Not for any absence of clouds. I can't be anyone— I haven't—
and tomorrow is not what you become effervescently. Is your name the
buttery sheathe of your wing unmarred?

An apparition found us, walking vividly through conspicuous clusters
of small— mostly in late summer—gravity— but also— we may— die
back to the ground.

We've pleaded applause. Why not remember— yourself? I know this
song is not what you've marred. I've not done enough on my last day
to perish. Peevish. Walk underwater. Caterwaul. Reply to the rabbit.
What have you read? I am climbing out of myself in a molted whisper.
And translate:

Yellow bird, yellow butterfly, we are her antidotes.

Phoebis

We match because we aren't supposed to be visible. You confuse us with shiny dark leaves, suites of insects.

She wore the yellow dress, yellow pearls, big as marbles, the color is rare. She shares our name. Only she could wear empathy, perfectly encircling her opposite birth.

Around her other—her— neck—platitude —given

And her other cannot read the shifting sands at the base of her pocketbook. Little wingspan of light held above.

Music forbidding, like a buttercup in a stage set of metal

Knowing one's body must burst. One's body isn't. A kerchief is not a sigh. A watermark never enters upstream. Fish are on the lawn.

I've seen this bleat and recombine. I have far too many words. And how to escort them — delicate membrane. We who are between— appalled. I know this song in which no one approaches her.

Psaltria

You disperse after the rains. You visit seep baccharis.

She begins so many things she disintegrates. Fly in and designate her edges, until she is someone else who writes about a bird. Her impulse is dispelling again with form, formlessness.

You are Phoebis for a bird, a moon, a genus.

She is going again, into the cave, chasm, before the next wave hits. What is a wave?

Phoebis, from Greek, Φοιβη, the radiant, please tell us. Why does she dream of water, while asleep in the desert, diving, too far out— before the next striking point?

She needs a place to be, as if being weren't caught on the yellow marble around her neck, a shell, something hidden in a book.

She is someone else now, not a person, who?

Phoebis

Your name is of psalmic. Why are we shadowing?

The place to go is only in the unconscious. She had written "on-conscious."
Is that equally a word or a wave? Is the unconscious a place? If she
doesn't have a companion she can go with the dead beloved. We describe
the shape of her imagined movement to the mourner. She is probably
busy but her dream image isn't busy.

Her gold or yellow or molten burnished dress is bright against the dank
of the dark. As if she wore light, reflected from her skin. Where— are
we going?

She begins to paint upon tin, sad little scenes pressed onto canvases. You
could call this an acreage of light. You could call this—you wouldn't
forget would you, that her body was no longer hers? She was somewhere
else—where "else" is immovable to us. She did not cry yesterday. That
seems a world. One day not to—no one approaches—and thought flew
out from her head like a bird.

Don't beckon. Don't. Begrudge. She wishes the long meter of time to
visit or interrupt and tell her when she might ever finish — distrusting
this absence.

Pull— from a lecture on seeds.

Psaltria

Somewhere, a place you can be, before the next wave hits. What is a wave?

Not a wave, she says pushing back her burnished, bright feathers (she has
no feathers, no wings— her gold or molten—was it her hair cascading to
her chin, or was it a gaze, gown upon gown of her outer breathing) —
breathing a little heavy. You are breathing a little —.

Don't worry, she says and she points up and down, where a body would
be, if she had one. You see— but it isn't my self. She speaks, but it isn't
her speaking from within the burnished outer reflection.

Where are you then, asks the other? What is a wave, she asks, unaware of
her own leaving.

It isn't a wave but what happens when I leave again. You cannot ask me
why because you know that you must keep yourself. She holds the other
she's hands, but never touches anything. You're - still - here, she says.
Almost an apology.

And you? Helen's sister, daughter of Leda, we are her antidotes. Which
her? Follow her. The one in body or the other?

Phoebis

If we keep telling this way, as if there were a dialogue, as if we followed a body— what is a wave— then how could anyone tell where, the other side of birth.

Are you there? Are you alright? I'm not believable. I also need a form —forewing, antenna, thorax.

Look, the daughter sits in her car, waiting for the schoolbus with her son. She reads him a tale or the morning paper. How old is the boy? He is any age, keeps changing. Her departed beloved floats in the palo verde watching. The boy looks up and says, look. You, Psaltria, soft yellow about the throat and crown. You peck at a blossom and sing.

He cannot see that you also adorn the wrist or the shoulder, her birth of loss. You flit to the mother's waist but attach yourself to a branch. Why is it we cannot be apart from her?

Psaltria

We share the same letter of the alphabet, feed upon seed heads, a ready supply of *tell me thy verse*, extracting and shelling shadows.

We are all three of us yellow— yellow pearl, yellow burnish, yellow blossom of palo verde.

Not a favorite color of either— she. The daughter tries on an immaterial garment, vanishes from view. She has never: turned to yellow, lit a candle in a house where there was no draft, fed a hen, noted flames leapt from a hearth, threw slivers of wood into air and read their fallen forms, interpreted a voice heard accidentally.

She wants to be sheathed in something, not color exactly, light possibly. Not warmth, the sun is too strong. Moon garment gather near and cover her— crying. Does a butterfly tire? Do a bird's wings fail?

Winsomely. Bothered. And beware of yourself.

Phoebis

Where are we going? Two roadrunners hurry across her thoughts, one after the other as if to dazzling plans. Hurry about as if destinations were actual—enactments.

Whose beautiful ballroom—desert floor, is it?

Her mourning is birth— in reverse. Near the time of death and immediately afterward— contractions are so close together she can barely breathe. When contractions come (waves) sensation is paralyzing. When they pass she is— briefly— almost herself.

As time lengthens away from loss waves crush further apart— but the immediacy- each time a wave arrives is completely— yellow. Harrowing isn't only beautiful, it is obligatory. Everything is borrowed.

Desire to enter time—it isn't— but mimics hunger— perforation of sight. What you see is no longer before you. A fictive countertop, more difficult than silt to contain. Why would such a clasp interfere with the imagined— absent nape?

Psaltria

She does not know how long anything lasts—passing—obligatory harrowing waves crushing. You could say winnowing, if she were chafe, hewn, risen and felled.

Contractions of mourning last longer —mourning waves— walk with her— and we will follow the invisible image she scries— having no endpoint, different durations and lengths between—. Nothing material comes though something immaterial is —.

A world permanently different with the beloved removed.

See the picture with a form cut out. She overlays it upon everything she sees, as if—pause— taking it out of blotter— but time doesn't stop so places instantaneously— doesn't know she walks within a self imposed frame— figure cut out. She sees an outline in silver on a map, hears a voice inside her head, considers how to steady herself, against what once was more than ether.

Phoebis

Illusion is that anything has changed, harrowed, departed. Hear the voice
inside her head bumping up against winnowed slivers of wood, waves, a
yellow borrowing of flight.

She arrives at her funeral party all over again, except that she, her
other "she" was there. She stood beside her, departed in lemon dress,
accompanied by yellow bird— yellow. A yellow butterfly encircled her
— this morning — as she walked.

The departed beloved could be seen by nobody— by her alone, and said:

Unbelievable, not to feel any pain. But then she narrowed her eyes and
spoke of how she was closing— her memory— in all of —these people—
finality.

Psaltria

She kept following me with her gaze, wondering, and where will you go now? Sometimes, like last night, she looks all around the room, and even out of doors, wondering where you are. As if, naturally she'd be able to see you hovering beside me. And she remembers your flying dreams— and how you can now- as a bird or a butterfly — and in ways we cannot imagine. She's supposed to be telling her dream.

You stand beside me and say, *you close the world to yourself, in every person's eyes. You end a relation.*

Yet relation goes on as disembodied yellow implores — in many forms— not to listen to this other self who stands beside a shade with no wing.

Rainbow Body in the Mirror of Death

Continuity of Mind

As our sun dies, what will happen to the planets
busy in second sight
Dung beetles dance a straight escape route
rest in naked awareness, always present
Bower birds take their names from elaborate grass structures
sheer immensity of a narrow way of thought
It was always the other emotion
Among many giant beasts such as the short-faced bear
we tell ourselves we want to spend time
with each choice secret to prevent infection
Arduous to carry marbles along rough roads
Nature of mind is too close, especially our own
Dewdrops form on the tips of grass blades
too vast for us to fathom

Ground Luminosity

In five billion years the earth will be engulfed
Experts cannot date the very first use of canal locks
I certainly understand the problem of last minute arrangements
straight and trim as the rash on a moss
burned up in the expanding radius of the sun
I am going out and when I return I shall not tell you
This appears to be in defiance of gravity
or a dance not contemplated with joy
Preparing a display of bones, shells, and stones
not wearing glass slippers
Sovereign cordials against corruption
endless activity of distraction

Path Luminosity

One million years after Venus and Mercury are absorbed by the sun
two heavy gates at the end of each basin
A request to turn off the digital read out
Drops accumulate randomly across the surface
and the soothsayer went forth out of the house
To avoid beetles that might want to steal their haul, insects must move
O nurse what cry is that?
A long avenue of bones and stones is prepared, creating an optical
illusion
When did instincts become extinct?
Who ran to conjurers, witches, blazing stars
looking naturally, at themselves

Opening of the Door

Long after the Earth becomes too hot to support life
a very skilled job for which dogs are trained is guiding the blind
You would not wish to repeat
the force that pulls water toward the smaller radius of the body
causes there a hillock, round and green
Beetles take compass readings from the sky
When the display is inverted birds will restore their entrances
to our everyday lives
Let them go by to the thicket
The smilodon is not related to any living cat or seamless ocean
nor any profane fellow or scoffer who wanders only to perish

Meeting of the Ground and Path Luminosity

As the sun ages into a red giant more loyal
and less nervous than purebred heavy rains
luminosity is sometimes incorrectly used to refer to luminance
Capillary effect is stronger than the force of gravity
and the image of the sun is very uncomfortable
The female bower bird makes her decision
One can see the bubbling surface in spots
based on presentation of the male's head
and the hole thus made to be covered over carefully
If you will not allow the bird benumbed with cold
the gathered will be dispersed
Nothing in them but air and vapour

Rainbow Body In the Mirror of Death

Tidal interaction of the sun and closely orbiting planets
models the behavior of two types of dewdrops:
A thin film of water and a thicker, spherical drop
Transportation is based on the use of ropes and pulleys
The beetles have four eyes before candle lighting
which is the density in a given direction.
As they roll away from the dung
their top eyes constantly watch the sky
Birds' art can be regarded in an aesthetic sense
because judgments are being made
Skin of swan and brindled red wave
Without the knowledge or suspicion of any living thing
apprehensions increase as errors
Impermanence is a parachute or a paragraphic intent

Illuminated Sleep Beneathe Trees

Gold nano particles make leaves glow in the dark

replace street lamps with trees laced—

Where goes bioluminescence by Fall?
as tree spirits C

A figure is lying out of doors, sleeping— beneathe—

In a solar spectrum you see only rustling, shaking
a face in shadow, body curled

Small ripened leaves fall and light up this portrait

The color of illuminated leaves varies
Light X amount in proportion

Turning bronze to register red furnace

Increasing length of night

Green pigment in leaves is bioluminescent
when exposed to high wavelength ultra violet excitation

Sea-urchin-shaped nanoparticles
excite chlorophyll to emit red light

Most of the verdance in sunlight is reflected
by leaves, greening them to our eyes

Trees lining roads luminescent at night

Your portrait returns as electromagnetic energy

Illuminated sleep provides a daguerreotype
emitted in a threefold spectrum:

Ultraviolet: invisible to the eye— spiritus, blast, breath, above blue
Visible: where you are now hidden— silvered copper plate
Infrared: vibrational coal stove —skin

The author is grateful to the editors of the following publications in which poems in this collection originally appeared: *Connotation Press: An Online Artifact* at www.connotationpress.com, *Delirious Hem* at delirioushem.blogspot.com, *Gulf Coast*, *InDigest*, Academy of American Poets, Poets.org (Poem-A-Day), *Spoon River Poetry Review*, *Spoke Too Soon*, and *Yew Journal* at yewjournal.com/aboutyew.html.

Endless thank you to Brad Davidson & to my family. Tremendous thanks to Kate Bernheimer, Lee Ann Brown, Lisa Jarnot, Bhanu Kapil, India Hixon, Pattie McCarthy, Claudia Rankine, Noah Saterstrom and Liz Willis for early readings and encouragement. Gratitude to everyone at Omnidawn, especially to Rusty Morrison, Ken Keegan and Gillian Hamel.

author photo by Joanna Eldredge Morrisey

Laynie Browne's most recent books include *P R A C T I C E* (SplitLevel 2015), *Scorpyn Odes* (Kore Press 2015) and *Lost Parkour Ps(alms)*, in two editions, one in English, and another in French (Presses universitaires de Rouen et du Havré 2014). Her honors include a 2014 Pew Fellowship, the National Poetry Series Award (2007) for her collection *The Scented Fox*, and the Contemporary Poetry Series Award (2005) for her collection *Drawing of a Swan Before Memory*. She teaches at University of Pennsylvania and at Swarthmore College.

You Envelop Me
by Laynie Browne

Cover Art by Noah Saterstrom
Natchez #1
Acrylic on paper, 9 x 12 inches, www.noahsaterstrom.com

Cover and interior set in Electra LT Std and Garamond 3 LT Std

Cover and interior design by Gillian Olivia Blythe Hamel

Offset printed in the United States
by Edwards Brothers Malloy, Ann Arbor, Michigan
On 55# Enviro Natural 100% Recycled 100% PCW
Acid Free Archival Quality FSC Certified Paper

Publication of this book was made possible in part by gifts from:
The Clorox Company
The New Place Fund
Robin & Curt Caton

Omnidawn Publishing
Oakland, California
2017
Rusty Morrison & Ken Keegan, senior editors & co-publishers
Gillian Olivia Blythe Hamel, managing editor
Cassandra Smith, poetry editor & book designer
Sharon Zetter, poetry editor, book designer & development officer
Avren Keating, poetry editor, fiction editor & marketing assistant
Liza Flum, poetry editor
Juliana Paslay, fiction editor
Gail Aronson, fiction editor
Trisha Peck, marketing assistant
Cameron Stuart, marketing assistant
Natalia Cinco, marketing assistant
Maria Kosiyanenko, marketing assistant
Emma Thomason, administrative assistant
SD Sumner, copyeditor
Kevin Peters, *OmniVerse* Lit Scene editor
Sara Burant, *OmniVerse* reviews editor